Dear Parents and Educators,

Welcome to Penguin Young Readers! As parents and educators, you know that each child develops at his or her own pace—in terms of speech, critical thinking, and, of course, reading. Penguin Young Readers recognizes this fact. As a result, each Penguin Young Readers book is assigned a traditional easy-to-read level (1–4) as well as a Guided Reading Level (A–P). Both of these systems will help you choose the right book for your child. Please refer to the back of each book for specific leveling information. Penguin Young Readers features esteemed authors and illustrators, stories about favorite characters, fascinating nonfiction, and more!

A Baby Panda Is Born

LEVEL **3**

GUIDED READING LEVEL **L**

This book is perfect for a **Transitional Reader** who:
- can read multisyllable and compound words;
- can read words with prefixes and suffixes;
- is able to identify story elements (beginning, middle, end, plot, setting, characters, problem, solution); and
- can understand different points of view.

Here are some **activities** you can do during and after reading this book:
- Compare/Contrast: In this book, the author says that "a panda is not your average bear." Using facts from this story, compare and contrast the panda to other bears.
- Research: The author writes that pandas are in danger. Research what you and your friends and family can do to try to protect these animals.

Remember, sharing the love of reading with a child is the best gift you can give!

—Bonnie Bader, EdM
  Penguin Young Readers program

*Penguin Young Readers are leveled by independent reviewers applying the standards developed by Irene Fountas and Gay Su Pinnell in *Matching Books to Readers: Using Leveled Books in Guided Reading*, Heinemann, 1999.

To my mother, who fostered in me a love
for all things cute 'n' fuzzy—KO

For my baby panda,
from mommy panda—LW

Penguin Young Readers
Published by the Penguin Group
Penguin Group (USA) Inc., 375 Hudson Street, New York, New York 10014, USA
Penguin Group (Canada), 90 Eglinton Avenue East, Suite 700, Toronto, Ontario M4P 2Y3, Canada
(a division of Pearson Penguin Canada Inc.)
Penguin Books Ltd, 80 Strand, London WC2R 0RL, England
Penguin Ireland, 25 St Stephen's Green, Dublin 2, Ireland (a division of Penguin Books Ltd)
Penguin Group (Australia), 707 Collins Street, Melbourne, Victoria 3008, Australia
(a division of Pearson Australia Group Pty Ltd)
Penguin Books India Pvt Ltd, 11 Community Centre, Panchsheel Park, New Delhi—110 017, India
Penguin Group (NZ), 67 Apollo Drive, Rosedale, Auckland 0632, New Zealand
(a division of Pearson New Zealand Ltd)
Penguin Books (South Africa), Rosebank Office Park, 181 Jan Smuts Avenue,
Parktown North 2193, South Africa
Penguin China, B7 Jiaming Center, 27 East Third Ring Road North,
Chaoyang District, Beijing 100020, China

Penguin Books Ltd, Registered Offices: 80 Strand, London WC2R 0RL, England

Text copyright © 2008 by Kristin Ostby. Illustrations copyright © 2008 by Lucia Washburn.
All rights reserved. First published in 2008 by Grosset & Dunlap, an imprint of Penguin Group (USA) Inc.
Published in 2013 by Penguin Young Readers, an imprint of Penguin Group (USA) Inc.,
345 Hudson Street, New York, New York 10014. Manufactured in China.

Library of Congress Control Number: 2007018783

ISBN 978-0-448-44720-9   10 9 8 7 6 5 4 3 2 1

A Baby Panda Is Born

by Kristin Ostby
illustrated by Lucia Washburn

Penguin Young Readers
An Imprint of Penguin Group (USA) Inc.

It is February 23, 2007.
From all over the world,
people have come to the zoo
in Atlanta.

There are TV crews and reporters. Why is everybody so excited?

Everyone wants to see
the new panda cub.

Her name is Mei Lan (say: May
Lahn).

Mei Lan is four months old.

But today is the first time
visitors will see her.

Mei Lan's mother is nearby.
She watches to make sure her
baby is safe.

Where is Mei Lan's
father? He lives in
another part of the zoo.
Mei Lan's mother
takes care of her cub
all by herself.

Mei Lan was born at the zoo.
At first, she was the size
of a stick of butter. Her body was
all pink with bits of white fuzz.
Her eyes were closed. She couldn't
see yet. She also cried a lot. She
sounded like a little piglet.

Two months later,
her eyes fully opened.

Her fur had turned black
in many places. The rest of her
fur was white.

Now she looked like a panda!

Being black and white
may help pandas blend
into the snow and dark rocks
of China. That's where all wild
pandas live.

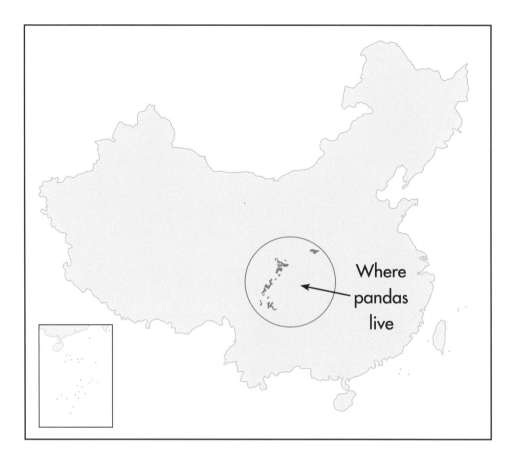

Where
pandas
live

China is a very big country.
Only Russia, Canada, and the
United States are bigger.

Pandas live in a very small
area of China. The circle shows
you where.

Mei Lan's name is Chinese.
It means "Atlanta beauty."
These are the Chinese
characters for her name.

Pandas are important to the
people of China.

Special gold and silver coins
have pictures of pandas on them.

This animal
is a red panda.
Red pandas also
live in China.

Red pandas are cousins
of giant pandas. But they
don't look much like them.
Red pandas look more
like raccoons.

Like most bears, pandas
like to climb trees.

Look how high
this panda can climb!
Up, up, up he goes!

Splash!

This panda just jumped
into the river.

Pandas are very good swimmers.
Most bears are.

But a panda is not
your average bear!
They weigh
no more than
250 pounds.

Panda
5 feet

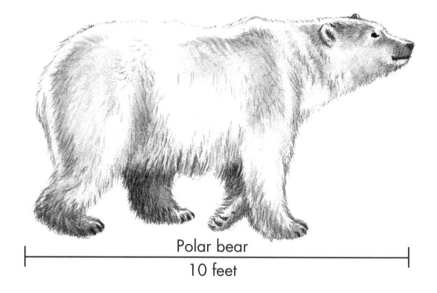

Polar bear
10 feet

Polar bears are much bigger.

Kodiak bear
10 feet

So are Kodiak bears.

Most bears sleep
through the cold winter.
But not pandas.
That is because it does
not get very cold in the part
of China where they live.

Most bears are meat eaters.
This grizzly bear is hunting
an elk.
Grizzlies also like to eat
fish and squirrels.

But pandas hardly
ever eat meat.
What do they like to eat?
Bamboo!

Bamboo is a type of long, hard grass. Pandas eat bamboo shoots and leaves. A panda can spend half its life eating! Can you imagine?

Pandas have special paws.
Each paw has five claws
plus an extra bone. It is sort of
like a thumb, but it can't bend
or move. Their special paws
help pandas hold bamboo.

Grizzly

Panda

At about six months old,
cubs start eating bamboo.

Before that, babies need only
their mothers' milk.

Mothers do their best
to protect their babies.
This panda mother
sees a jackal. She growls to
scare him away.
She must also watch out
for leopards.

In China, there are probably around 1,600 pandas in the wild. That's not very many.

In the last few years, more pandas have been born in zoos and nature reserves. That's why everyone was so excited about Mei Lan.

Why are there so few pandas in the wild?

CANADA
33 million

GREENLAND
56 thousand

USA
301 million

BRAZIL
188 million

One reason is that so many people live in China—more than one billion.

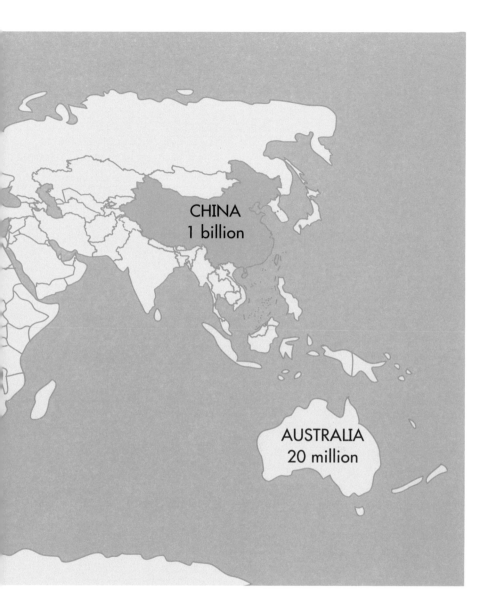

That's way more than in any other country in the world.

In China, more and more homes
are built near where pandas live.

Pandas are very shy animals.
They are afraid to look for
bamboo near people's homes.

So some pandas can't
find enough food to eat.

There are new laws
to protect pandas.

People can't build houses
too close to where they live.

People can't hunt
pandas anymore.

Anyone who kills
a panda is sent to jail
for a long time.

At the zoo in Atlanta, Mei Lan will always have plenty of food.

And she will always be safe.

Is she lonely with no other panda cubs?

No.

She likes to climb and explore.

All she needs is her mother.

But in a few years,
she will be fully grown.
Then she will be ready to have
a panda cub of her own!
For now she loves lying
in her hammock in the sun.